Bible 5 Journal

Moses • First Christmas • Joshua
Judges • Ruth • Jonah • Samuel • David

MW01714878

This Journal Belongs To:

Write Name Here

abeka
Pensacola, FL 32523-9100
an affiliate of PENSACOLA CHRISTIAN COLLEGE®

To Parents and Teachers

Bible 5 Journal, correlated with the Grade 5 Bible Flash-a-Card series, provides a unique opportunity for personal application and biblical worldview development.

Because personal philosophy and perception of truth is the framework that guides our choices and interactions with God and others, it is of utmost importance to teach and encourage the development of a biblical worldview within the heart and mind of each student. This development begins with instruction in the foundational truths of the Word of God and leads to application in daily living. Following the instruction of these truths in the daily Bible lessons, this journal provides additional opportunity for students to develop their personal biblical worldview through a variety of discussion questions.

The weekly journal entry guides students not only in the recall of Bible lesson facts, but also in personal application of the accompanying biblical principles. Each lesson series concludes with the Assemblage Analysis, tying the series together with important takeaway thoughts and biblical application questions. The final pages include a Creative Writing/Profile Drawing section, allowing students to creatively consider an aspect from the lessons. Puzzles or decorative verse pages highlight lessons learned in the series. Throughout this journal, students practically and personally apply Scripture and the truths they are learning. Encourage students to share their thoughts through guided discussions as you informally assess their understanding of the lessons and truths covered.

Bible 5 Journal

Staff Credits
Author: Faith Nulph
Managing Editor: Amy Yohe
Product Manager: Barbie Tupua
Designer: Karen Kisner
Illustrators: Jeremy Gorman, Peter Kothe, Margaret Benson, Dakotah Cort, Joshua Burylo, Emma Watson, and Abeka Staff

Credits: images used throughout: phokin/Getty Images, RussellTate/Getty Images

Salvation Story
Promise of God

Salvation Story

Entry 1

Bible Reading

- > Revelation 21:10–22
- > Genesis 3:1–6
- > John 18:28–40
- > John 19:1–16
- > Matthew 28:1–10

Beneath the Surface

A *precept* is a lesson, a command, or a principle used to guide decisions regarding behavior. God wants you to look for or listen for His precepts as you read, study, and hear His Word.

Think about **Psalm 119:4** as you copy it in the space below.

What word in this verse tells you that it will take commitment to keep God's precepts?

Looking Back

The precept from this week's lessons that I want to apply to my life is . . .

I can apply that precept by . . .

Observations

Read **Genesis 1:3, 26–27,** and **2:7**. Name one way that the creation of man was different from the creation of the world.

Read **Genesis 2:8–9**. Where did God place Adam and Eve?

Read **Genesis 3:1**. How did Satan influence Eve's thinking about God?

How might the things of the world influence your thinking about God?

Eve began to question the truth of God's Word. What else did Eve's questioning lead to?

Does Satan want you to question the truth of God's Word?

What else does Satan want you to question?

Read **Numbers 23:19** and **Proverbs 30:5**. How does knowing that God does not lie strengthen your faith in His Word?

What is one thing that Jesus did while He was on Earth that proved He was God?

Why did Jesus come to Earth?

Daily Living

- This week I want to thank God for...
- This week I want to serve others by...
- This week when I think of others, I want to remember to pray for...
- The missionary I want to pray for this week is...
- I want to ask God to help me...

NEVER DOUBT
the truth of God's Word.

So teach us to
number our days,
that we may apply
our hearts
unto wisdom.
Psalm 90:12

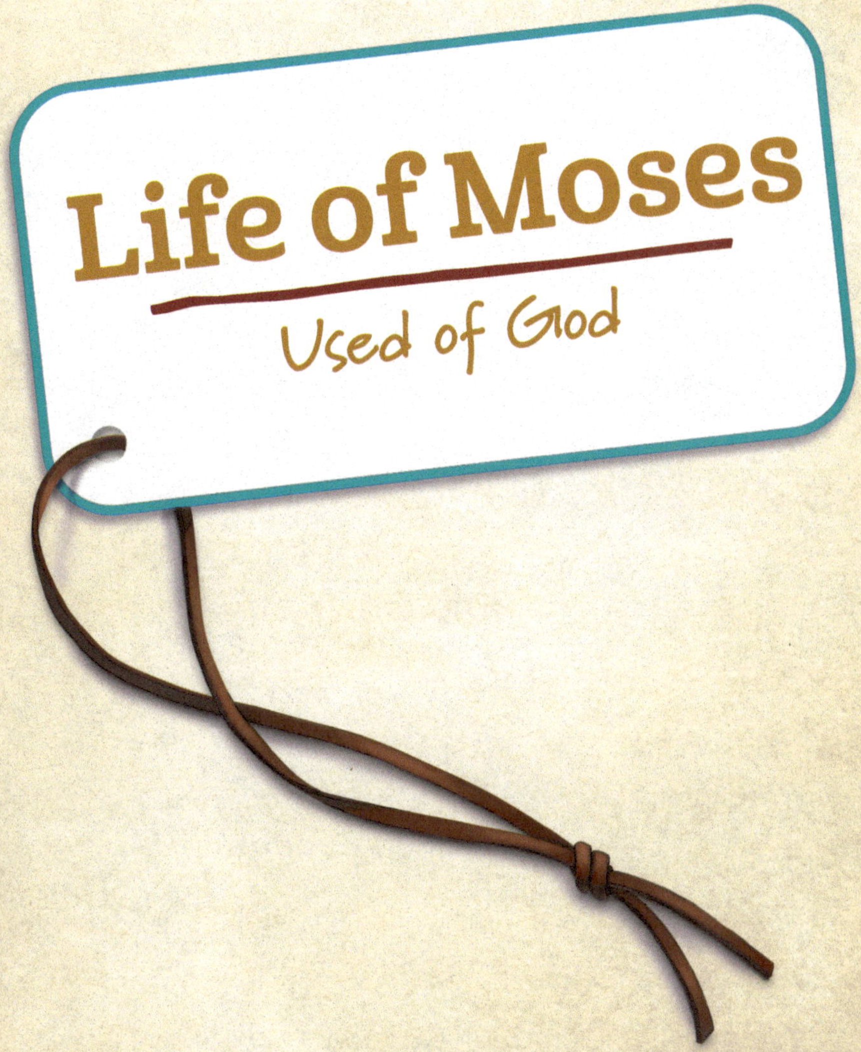
Life of Moses
Used of God

Life of Moses
Entry 1

Bible Reading

- Exodus 1:1–14
- Exodus 2:5–15
- Exodus 2:16–25
- Exodus 3:1–22
- Exodus 4:1–17

Beneath the Surface

Think about **Hebrews 11:25–26** as you *finish* the verses in the space below.

"Choosing rather to suffer affliction with the people of God, than to enjoy the pleasures of sin for a season;

Why did Moses choose to leave the palace and riches of Egypt?

Looking Back

A *precept* is a lesson, a command, or a principle used to guide decisions regarding behavior.

The precept from this week's lessons that I want to apply to my life is . . .

I can apply that precept by . . .

Observations

Read **Genesis 15:13–14**. What promise, given to Abraham, gave the Israelites hope as they lived in slavery?

Read **Exodus 2:8–9**. How did God reward Jochebed's faith when she placed Moses in the basket?

Being under the control of the Egyptians was difficult for the Israelites. Read **Nahum 1:7**. What promises do you find in this verse that would help you during a difficult time?

Moses would have received a good education and learned some leadership skills growing up in the palace. Read **Proverbs 8:11**. What else did Moses need to learn from God to lead the people of Israel?

What can help prepare you for God's plan for your life?

Read **Exodus 3:4–5**. After forty years in the wilderness, where did God meet with Moses?

Why did God tell him to take off his shoes?

How might thinking about God's holiness help you concentrate as you read His Word?

Daily Living

- This week I want to thank God for...
- This week I want to serve others by...
- This week when I think of others, I want to remember to pray for...
- The family member I want to pray for this week is...
- I want to ask God to help me...

FOCUS on the One through Whom you can do ALL things.

Life of Moses
Entry 2

Bible Reading

- Exodus 5:1–13; 6:1–8
- Exodus 7:8–22
- Exodus 8:9–22
- Exodus 9:5–12, 18–21
- Exodus 10:1–11, 21–26

Beneath the Surface

Think about **Exodus 7:5** as you copy it in the space below.

What did God want the Egyptians to learn through the plagues?

Looking Back

The precept from this week's lessons that I want to apply to my life is . . .

I can apply that precept by . . .

Observations

Read **Exodus 4:31**. When the leaders of Israel first heard that they would be delivered from Egypt, "they bowed their heads and ________________."

Read **Exodus 5:20–22**. When things got worse, the Israelites responded in anger toward ________________ and ________________.

Moses responded by taking his questions to ________________.

Read **Exodus 6:6–8**. How many times did God say "I will" in these verses?

Do you think this encouraged Moses and the Israelites?
Why or why not?

Read **Exodus 7:10–12**. How was Aaron's rod different from the rods of the magicians?

Read **Exodus 8:17–18**. What was the first plague the Egyptians could not imitate?

Why do you think that Satan sometimes imitates what God does?

Read **John 8:31–32**. How can you know the difference between the truth of God and the deception of Satan?

Read **Exodus 8:21–22**. What was the plague that separated the Israelites from the Egyptians?

Daily Living

- This week I want to thank God for...
- This week I want to serve others by...
- This week when I think of others, I want to remember to pray for...
- The church worker I want to pray for this week is...
- I want to ask God to help me...

IMITATION is never as good as the REAL THING.

Life of Moses
Entry 3

Bible Reading

- Exodus 11:1–10
- Exodus 12:1–5, 11–14
- Exodus 12:22–36
- Exodus 13:19–14:18
- Exodus 14:19–31

Beneath the Surface

Think about **Exodus 14:13–14** as you *finish* by writing verse 14 in the space below.

"And Moses said unto the people, Fear ye not, stand still, and see the salvation of the Lord, which He will show to you today: . . . The Lord shall

Why should you not be anxious or worried when you are waiting for God to work in a situation?

Looking Back

The precept from this week's lessons that I want to apply to my life is . . .

I can apply that precept by . . .

Observations

Read **Exodus 12:5, 11**. During the Passover meal, why was it so important that the lamb be without blemish or spot?

Read **Hebrews 10:12**. Why did the offering of the lamb stop after Jesus died on the cross?

We no longer offer a sacrifice for our sins, but the Bible does tell us what we can offer to God. In your own words, explain **Romans 12:1**.

The Israelites were to eat their meal dressed and ready so that when the call came, they were ready to leave. Read **1 Thessalonians 4:16–17**. How can you be ready for the Lord's return?

Read **Exodus 13:21–22**. How did the Lord lead Israel when they left Egypt?

Today God leads you with His Word. You probably take it with you when you go to church. How often do you read it throughout the rest of the week?

God's Word cannot lead you if you do not read it. What opportunities do you have this week to learn from God's Word?

Read **Exodus 14:10–14**. How did the Israelites react when they reached the Red Sea and knew Pharaoh's army was coming?

How and **why** was Moses' reaction different?

Read **Exodus 14:15**. Why would God tell the people to go forward before the Red Sea had parted?

Would you have wanted to be at the front of the line taking that step of faith toward the Red Sea?
Why or why not?

Life of Moses
Assemblage Analysis

As archaeologists study artifacts, they group the items together to study what they have uncovered. This process is called Assemblage Analysis. As you are studying the Bible, consider the truths, ask questions, gather verses, think about what they mean, pray for understanding; and God will show you how to live for Him each day.

Analysis 1

God used the palace and the desert to prepare Moses to lead His people. What might have been one lesson Moses learned either in the palace or in the desert?

What lesson has God taught you recently?

Analysis 2

God spoke to Moses from a burning bush. God may speak to you through a sermon, your daily Bible study, a particular verse, or a missionary presentation. What will you say to God when you know what He wants you to do?

Read **Philippians 4:13**. What assurance do you have that you will be able to do what God calls you to do?

Analysis 3

Read **Exodus 8:8–10**. Why do you think Pharaoh told Moses to take the frogs away "tomorrow" instead of immediately?

Sometimes you may choose to continue in sin even when you know it is wrong. Why should you take care of sin immediately?

Analysis 4

God told Moses to leave and take His people to the Promised Land. Pharaoh offered compromises to Moses which would keep the Israelites close to Egypt. Read **Exodus 8:25, 28** and **10:11, 24**. Why do you think it was important for the Israelites to go all the way to the Promised Land?

Read **2 Corinthians 6:17–18**, **Colossians 3:1–2**, and **2 Timothy 2:4**. Why do you think that Satan wants you to stay close to worldly desires and worldly thinking?

Creative Writing

Write a selection comparing and contrasting an Egyptian's and an Israelite's reaction to one of the plagues. You may choose any of the plagues. Write a paragraph of similarities and a paragraph of differences. You may choose to use some of these signal words:

however, both, although, different, similar, alike

continue on next page

Profile Drawing

Try sketching an illustration of your story in the space below.

Profile Drawing is an archaeological term for a cross-section drawing representing the excavation walls.

The next day John seeth *Jesus* coming unto him, *and saith*, Behold *the Lamb of God*, which taketh away *the sin of the* world.

John 1:29

Life of Moses
Entry 4

Bible Reading

- Exodus 15:22–27
- Exodus 16:1–9
- Exodus 16:10–21
- Exodus 16:27–36
- John 6:26–40

Beneath the Surface

Think about **Exodus 16:15** as you copy it in the space below.

How did manna demonstrate God's attribute of love?

Looking Back

The precept from this week's lessons that I want to apply to my life is . . .

I can apply that precept by . . .

Observations

Read **Exodus 15:22–25**. How long did the Israelites travel to Marah?

To prove something is to test it. How did God test the faith of the people at Marah?

Instead of murmuring, what should the Israelites have done?

How can you help yourself focus on your blessings when you are tempted to complain?

Read **Exodus 16:7–8**. When the people complained to Moses or about Moses, whom were they really complaining about?

How did God take care of the Israelites' need for food?

Read **John 6:35**. How was manna a picture of Jesus?

How can you find nourishment from the Bread of Life?

Read **Exodus 16:35**. How long did the manna last?

Throughout Exodus 15 and 16, what attribute of God is most evident?

Daily Living

- This week I want to thank God for...
- This week I want to serve others by...
- This week when I think of others, I want to remember to pray for...
- The government official I want to pray for this week is...
- I want to ask God to help me...

During difficult times,

TURN TO GOD

not from Him.

Life of Moses
Entry 5

Bible Reading

- > Exodus 17:1–12
- > Psalm 106:7–13
- > Psalm 107:1–9
- > Psalm 136:1–12
- > Psalm 136:13–26

Beneath the Surface

Think about **1 John 4:4** as you copy it in the space below.

Who will help you to have spiritual victory in your life?

Looking Back

The precept from this week's lessons that I want to apply to my life is . . .

I can apply that precept by . . .

Observations

Did God have a plan when He led the people to a place with no water?

Read **Psalm 139:1–4**. How do you know God has a plan for your life?

Read **Exodus 17:2**. What does *chide* mean?

If you had been Moses, what would you have said to the people when they complained?

What did God do for the people when they needed water?

How do you think you may have responded if you had seen this miracle?

Read **1 Corinthians 10:4** and **Isaiah 53:10**. The rock that Moses struck is a picture of _______________ when He died on the cross.

Joshua, Moses, Aaron, and Hur each had a responsibility in the battle with the Amalekites. Read **Exodus 17:9–13**. Who gave the victory?

What if one person had decided not to do his part? How might things have been different?

What responsibilities do you have that will prepare you to follow God's plan for your life?

Daily Living

- This week I want to thank God for...
- This week I want to serve others by...
- This week when I think of others, I want to remember to pray for...
- The friend I want to pray for this week is...
- I want to ask God to help me...

REMEMBERING how GOD helped YOU in the PAST is an important part of YOUR FUTURE.

Life of Moses

Entry 6

Bible Reading

- > Exodus 19:1–11
- > Exodus 19:16–25
- > Exodus 24:12–18
- > Exodus 32:1–13
- > Exodus 20:1–17

Beneath the Surface

Think about **Exodus 19:4** as you copy it in the space below.

Read **Romans 5:8**. Before you understood that you are a sinner, God ________________ you.

Looking Back

The precept from this week's lessons that I want to apply to my life is . . .

I can apply that precept by . . .

Observations

Read **Exodus 19:8** and **24:3**. Did the people actually do what they promised while Moses was on the mountain?

Read **John 14:15, 21**. Why is it important for you to obey God's Word?

The people prepared themselves and their camp for the coming of God. Read **Exodus 19:10–11**. How can you prepare your heart before reading your Bible or going to church?

Read **Exodus 32:1–4**. What did Aaron do while Moses was gone?

Did Aaron know that what he was doing for the people was wrong?

Why do you think Aaron went along with the people right away?

Is it easy to do right when everyone around you is trying to persuade you to do wrong? Why or why not?

What do you think Aaron should have said to the people?

Read **Exodus 32:21–24**. When Moses returned, did Aaron take responsibility for what he had done?

Do you take responsibility when you do wrong?

When God wanted to destroy the people for their sin, Moses prayed. Read **Exodus 32:31–32**. What can you learn from Moses' prayer?

Read **Galatians 3:24–25**. What was the purpose of the law that was given to Moses?

Who is the only one able to obey or keep all of the law?

Since the resurrection, Christians worship on the first day of the week. What is one way you can keep that day different from the other days of the week?

How can you honor your mother and father?

Read **Exodus 20:16**. What does it mean to bear false witness against your neighbor?

You hear someone telling untruths about someone and you know the truth. Explain *what* you should do and *why* it would be the right thing to do.

Analysis 1

When the people of Israel faced problems, how did they consistently respond?

How did Moses consistently respond?

Read **Colossians 3:17**. What is the biblical response to all situations?

Analysis 2

Do you think practicing some good responses would help you develop good habits?

Maybe you could start with some of these. "I would be glad to do that for you." "I'm so glad we have plenty of food to eat each day." "Thank you for reminding me." What are some other good responses you could practice or begin saying when you might feel like complaining?

Analysis 3

Read **Psalm 103:1**. How is God's name described in this verse?

God says not to use His name in ________________.

Read **Philippians 2:9–11**. What does the Bible tell you about the name of Jesus?

Read **John 14:13**. What is one thing you can do in God's name?

Analysis 4

What does it mean to covet?

Read **Philippians 4:11**. How could you keep from coveting?

Creative Writing

Pretend you are an Israelite. Write what you would think, do, or say when there was no water at Rephidim. Remember to use the words *I* and *we* to write from this point of view.

For example, you would write something like this:

We have followed Moses and now he brings us to a place where there is no water. God has always supplied our needs. I wonder what He will do this time.

continue on next page

Profile Drawing

Try sketching an illustration of your story in the space below.

Word Search

Find and circle the words from the word bank. Cross them off the list when you find them. Words can be across, down, or diagonal.

T	A	K	C	S	L	D	E	T	H	H	A	H	Q	W	O
S	E	H	L	M	U	R	M	U	R	Y	O	Q	O	Z	S
L	K	N	N	W	E	I	U	P	O	A	S	N	R	N	T
D	F	C	C	Z	W	N	R	M	U	N	R	C	O	A	O
J	G	T	Y	O	I	S	W	P	I	M	S	Y	M	R	N
M	K	W	R	S	M	T	Y	U	I	O	P	F	O	H	E
A	A	R	O	N	E	M	J	D	S	W	E	Y	S	I	T
N	R	D	S	I	S	R	A	E	L	W	A	M	E	F	A
N	G	F	R	D	H	Y	T	N	I	O	P	Y	S	M	B
A	M	L	P	N	K	O	B	H	D	U	V	G	Y	I	L
T	X	D	R	Z	S	E	Q	W	A	M	P	L	M	R	E
N	I	T	A	B	E	R	N	A	C	L	E	U	H	I	T
L	E	G	Y	P	T	G	V	R	F	C	E	N	D	A	S
S	A	Z	E	S	A	W	Q	Z	A	Q	W	S	T	M	D
C	R	W	F	V	T	G	R	O	C	K	B	Y	H	S	U
J	G	R	A	C	E	L	P	S	A	B	B	A	T	H	P

- Aaron
- Egypt
- grace
- honor
- Israel
- law
- manna
- Miriam
- Moses
- murmur
- rock
- Sabbath
- stone tablets
- Tabernacle
- Ten Commandments

Tabernacle
Entry 7

Bible Reading

- Exodus 25:1–16
- Exodus 26:1–13
- Exodus 27:9–21
- Exodus 30:1–10, 18–21
- Exodus 40:17–38

Beneath the Surface

Think about **Psalm 119:133** as you copy it in the space below.

Why is it important to ask God to guide your steps?

Looking Back

The precept from this week's lessons that I want to apply to my life is . . .

I can apply that precept by . . .

Observations

Read **Exodus 25:1–2, 8**. What did God ask the people to do so that the Tabernacle could be built?

What was the purpose of the Tabernacle?

Read **John 14:16–17**. Where does God the Holy Spirit dwell today?

Read **John 10:9**. How was the Tabernacle entrance a picture of Jesus?

The oil in the candlestick represented the Holy Spirit. How does the Holy Spirit help you as you read the Word of God?

What might the Holy Spirit bring to mind when you are faced with a difficult decision?

Read **Exodus 25:21**. What was the lid on the Ark of the Covenant called?

Read **Hebrews 9:7**. How often was the High Priest permitted to enter the Holy of Holies?

Read **Matthew 27:51**. When Jesus died on the cross, what happened to the curtain that divided the Holy Place from the Holy of Holies?

Because we have access to God the Father through Jesus, what things should become natural behavior for those who have trusted in Jesus?

Ark of the Covenant

Daily Living

- This week I want to thank God for...
- This week I want to serve others by...
- This week when I think of others, I want to remember to pray for...
- The first responders I want to pray for this week are...
- I want to ask God to help me...

ONLY through JESUS can YOU ENTER into the presence of the Holy God.

Life of Moses

Entry 8

Bible Reading

- > Numbers 10:29–36
- > Numbers 11:1–23
- > Numbers 12:1–8, 13
- > Numbers 13:1–3, 21–33
- > Numbers 14:1–24

Beneath the Surface

Think about **Matthew 11:29** as you copy it in the space below.

How is Christ described in this verse?

Looking Back

The precept from this week's lessons that I want to apply to my life is . . .

I can apply that precept by . . .

Observations

Read **Numbers 11:1–3**. According to this verse, what displeased the Lord?

What consequence did God send as a result of their sin?

Read **Numbers 11:16–17**. When Moses felt overwhelmed, how did God help him?

Read **Numbers 11:31**. What meat did God send in answer to their complaining about the food?

Read **Numbers 12:13**. How did Moses react when Miriam was punished?

Read **Numbers 13:27–28**. What does the word *nevertheless* mean?

Which of the spies showed great faith in God?

How did God reward their faith?

What is one way God will reward your faith?

Before the Israelites left Egypt, God said He would give them the land of Canaan. What attribute of God should have given them the assurance that they would conquer the land?

Read **Deuteronomy 1:29–31**. How did Moses react when the people refused to go into the Promised Land?

Daily Living

- This week I want to thank God for...
- This week I want to serve others by...
- This week when I think of others, I want to remember to pray for...
- The family member I want to pray for this week is...
- I want to ask God to help me...

Your spiritual strength will grow as you exercise the MUSCLES OF GRATITUDE.

Life of Moses

Entry 9

Bible Reading

- > Numbers 16:1–7, 12–14, 25–30, 41
- > Numbers 17:1–9
- > Numbers 20:1–13
- > Numbers 20:14–22
- > Numbers 20:23–29

Beneath the Surface

Think about **Jeremiah 29:11** as you copy it in the space below.

God's thoughts toward you are peaceful and hopeful. How does that affect your outlook on today?

Looking Back

The precept from this week's lessons that I want to apply to my life is . . .

I can apply that precept by . . .

Observations

Who called Moses to lead the people of Israel, Aaron to be the high priest, and the tribe of Levi to be in charge of the Tabernacle?

Korah, Dathan, and Abiram criticized Moses and Aaron's leadership. Read **Numbers 16:9–10**. What did they want for themselves?

Instead of complaining, how could you handle a difference between you and someone in authority?

Read **Numbers 16:41**. After God punished Korah, Dathan, and Abiram, how long was it before the Israelites complained again?

Read **Numbers 20:1–3**. Who died in the desert of Zin?

The Israelites saw God miraculously supply their daily needs for many years. Why do you think they still complained when they again had no water?

Read **Numbers 20:8, 11**. What instructions did God give to Moses regarding the rock?

Read **Hebrews 10:10–12**. How did Moses' disobedience ruin the picture of Jesus dying on the cross?

Why were Moses and Aaron not allowed to go into the Promised Land?

Daily Living

- This week I want to thank God for...
- This week I want to serve others by...
- This week when I think of others, I want to remember to pray for...
- The church worker I want to pray for this week is...
- I want to ask God to help me...

EACH TIME you read a promise of God, STOP AND THINK how it is true in YOUR LIFE.

Life of Moses
Entry 10

Bible Reading

- Numbers 21:4–9
- John 3:14–18
- Numbers 22:1–12
- Numbers 22:13–19
- Numbers 22:20–35

Beneath the Surface

Think about **John 3:17** as you copy it in the space below.

How would you respond to someone who says that they do not need a relationship with God?

Looking Back

The precept from this week's lessons that I want to apply to my life is . . .

I can apply that precept by . . .

Observations

Read **Numbers 21:9**. When God sent fiery serpents to punish the Israelites, what was the only way the people could be healed?

Read **John 3:14–16**. How was the brass pole a picture of Jesus dying on the cross?

Read **Numbers 21:17**. When the Israelites began to trust what God said, they stopped complaining and started to

________________.

Read **Numbers 22:6**. What did Balak want Balaam to do?

Read **Numbers 22:17**. What persuaded Balaam to go to Balak?

Balaam knew what God said, but he chose to focus on what Balak offered him. Read **Colossians 3:2**. How could daily focusing upon God help you to make wise decisions for your future?

Read **Numbers 23:19**. What does this verse tell you about God?

After hearing God's word from the angel, what did Balaam do when he saw the Israelites?

Throughout your life, you will make thousands of decisions. Some will be very easy to make, and others will require thought. Read **James 1:5–6**. How can you know the right thing to do?

What did God tell Balaam when he asked about going to Balak?

Daily Living

- This week I want to thank God for...

- This week I want to serve others by...

- This week when I think of others, I want to remember to pray for...

- The government official I want to pray for this week is...

- I want to ask God to help me...

OBEYING GOD *is always the* **RIGHT THING** *to do.*

Life of Moses
Entry 11

Bible Reading

- Numbers 27:12–23
- Deuteronomy 3:23–28; 4:5–10
- Deuteronomy 31:2–6
- Deuteronomy 34:1–12
- Luke 9:28–36

Beneath the Surface

Think about **Deuteronomy 31:6** as you copy it in the space below.

Why did Moses tell the people not to be afraid as they journeyed into the Promised Land?

Looking Back

The precept from this week's lessons that I want to apply to my life is . . .

I can apply that precept by . . .

Observations

Think about the verse you copied, **Deuteronomy 31:6**, as you answer the next question. How did Moses, whom God described as "very meek," lead millions of people through the wilderness for over forty years?

Could God call you to do something that you do not feel qualified to do?

Would you be willing to do anything God asks you to do?

What books of the Bible did Moses write?

God had forgiven Moses for his disobedience, but there was still a consequence. Read **Deuteronomy 3:23–27**. Why do you think Moses asked God to allow him to go into the Promised Land?

What was God's answer to Moses' request?

Read **Deuteronomy 34:1–4**. What did God allow Moses to do before he died?

According to **Deuteronomy 31:2**, how old was Moses the last time he spoke to the people of Israel?

Read **Deuteronomy 34:10–12**. In your own words, what did God say about Moses after Moses died?

Read **Matthew 17:1–3**. Many years after Moses died, he was seen in the Promised Land. When does the Bible say that he was there?

Whom did God choose to lead the Israelites after Moses' death?

Joshua ministered to Moses for 40 years. How do you think this prepared Joshua for leadership?

Analysis 1

God performed many miracles throughout Moses' life. Name one of these miracles you would like to have seen and write what lesson you learned from it.

Analysis 2

Joshua ministered to or helped Moses. What are some tasks that you could do to help others?

Read **Mark 10:43, 45**. What did Jesus teach about ministering to others when He was on Earth?

Analysis 3

As you think about Moses and the Israelites, what have you learned about murmuring and complaining?

What might you do or say to help stop the complaining?

Analysis 4

If you could ask Moses one question, what would you ask him?

How do you think he would answer?

Creative Writing

Choose an event in the life of Moses to write about. Simply retell Moses' experience in your own words. You, the author, will not refer to yourself or be included. For example, you would write something like this:

The Israelites were excited to leave slavery and be on their way to the Promised Land. Excitement quickly changed to panic when the people realized that the Red Sea was in front of them and the Egyptians were coming behind them. What would Moses do next?

continue on next page

Profile Drawing

Try sketching an illustration of your story in the space below.

Maze

First Christmas

Son of God

Christmas
Entry 1

Bible Reading

- Matthew 1:18–23
- Matthew 2:1–15
- Luke 1:26–38
- Luke 2:8–20
- Luke 2:25–38

Beneath the Surface

Think about **1 John 4:14** as you copy it in the space below.

Why did God send His Son to the world?

Looking Back

The precept from this week's lessons that I want to apply to my life is . . .

I can apply that precept by . . .

Observations

What did God promise Adam after he sinned in the Garden of Eden?

Read Luke 2:10–11. Why do you think the angel described the birth of Jesus as "great joy, which shall be to all people"?

Why do you think that the angels announced Jesus' birth to the shepherds first?

Read Luke 2:17–18. What does it mean that the shepherds "made known abroad the saying which was told them"?

How can you be a part of telling others about Jesus today?

Read Luke 2:19. What does it mean that Mary "pondered them in her heart"?

As you read God's Word, do you take the time to ponder what you read?

Read Matthew 2:2–3. Why did the Wise Men come to see Jesus?

Why was Herod troubled when he was asked, "Where is He that is born King of the Jews?"

Daily Living

- This week I want to thank God for...
- This week I want to serve others by...
- This week when I think of others, I want to remember to pray for...
- The first responders I want to pray for this week are...
- I want to ask God to help me...

Make JESUS the focus of your CHRISTMAS.

What Christmas Means to Me

Joshua

Warrior for God

Joshua
Entry 1

Bible Reading

- Numbers 27:15–23
- Deuteronomy 33:26–29
- Joshua 1:1–9
- Joshua 1:10–18
- Joshua 2:1–15, 21–24

Beneath the Surface

Think about **Joshua 1:9** as you copy it in the space below.

What gives you courage to serve God?

Looking Back

The precept from this week's lessons that I want to apply to my life is . . .

I can apply that precept by . . .

Observations

Read **Numbers 14:6–9**. What kind of report did Joshua give when he spied out the land of Canaan?

Read **Numbers 27:18–20**. What instructions did God give to Moses regarding Joshua?

Read **Matthew 20:27–28**. What principle did Jesus give us for leadership?

Name one way Joshua served Israel before he became the new leader.

Read **Deuteronomy 31:8**. How did Moses encourage Joshua when he became the new leader of Israel?

Read **Joshua 1:8**. According to God's Word, how can you be successful in your life?

Read **Joshua 2:9–11**. Why do you think Rahab helped the spies?

How did Rahab and the people of Jericho know about the God of Israel?

Where did Rahab hide the spies?

Whom else was Rahab concerned about?

Daily Living

- This week I want to thank God for...
- This week I want to serve others by...
- This week when I think of others, I want to remember to pray for...
- The missionary I want to pray for this week is...
- I want to ask God to help me...

A SUCCESSFUL LEADER SERVES those he is called to lead.

Joshua
Entry 2

Bible Reading

- Joshua 3:1–7, 14–17
- Joshua 5:10–15; 6:1–5
- Joshua 6:6–20
- Joshua 7:1–15
- Joshua 8:1–13

Beneath the Surface

Think about **1 John 5:4** as you copy it in the space below.

How does God describe victory in this verse?

Looking Back

The precept from this week's lessons that I want to apply to my life is . . .

I can apply that precept by . . .

Observations

Read **Joshua 3:15–16**. When did God stop the water of the Jordan River from flowing?

Read **Joshua 5:15**. Who came to give Joshua instructions for Jericho?

Jericho was the first city conquered in the Promised Land. Read **Joshua 6:19**. What were the Israelites instructed to do with the spoils of the city?

Read **Proverbs 3:9**. How could you give God the first part of something in your life?

Read **Joshua 7:2–3**. When the men returned from looking at Ai, what did they advise Joshua to do?

Read **Joshua 7:6–9**. How did Joshua react to the first battle of Ai?

Why do you think God waited to reveal Achan's sin?

Read **Joshua 7:21**. What was the progression of Achan's sin from when he saw the riches of Jericho until he hid them in his tent?

Read **Philippians 4:11**. Achan saw and coveted the riches of Jericho. What is one way to guard against coveting?

Daily Living

- This week I want to thank God for...
- This week I want to serve others by...
- This week when I think of others, I want to remember to pray for...
- The family member I want to pray for this week is...
- I want to ask God to help me...

LOOKING at the wrong thing often leads to desiring the wrong thing. DESIRING the wrong thing often leads to PARTICIPATING in the wrong thing.

Joshua
Entry 3

Bible Reading

- > Joshua 9:1–15
- > Joshua 9:16–21
- > Joshua 9:22–27
- > Joshua 10:1–11
- > Joshua 10:12–27

Beneath the Surface

Think about **Psalm 119:29** as you copy it in the space below.

How does the desire of the psalmist's heart differ from the tactics of the Gibeonites?

Looking Back

The precept from this week's lessons that I want to apply to my life is . . .

I can apply that precept by . . .

Observations

Why did the men of Gibeon want to trick the Israelites?

Why were Joshua and the men of Israel so easily deceived by the men of Gibeon?

Read **Joshua 10:8**. What gave Joshua courage for the battle with the five kings?

Read **Joshua 10:12–13**. How did God show His omnipotence in this battle?

Read **Romans 8:31**. What does this verse mean to you?

Read **Joshua 10:14**. How did God honor Joshua's faith?

The mustard seed is one of the smallest seeds, and yet it can grow into one of the largest plants. Read **Matthew 17:20**. Why do you think God used a mustard seed to describe faith in this verse?

Is there anything too big or small for you to pray about?

Daily Living

- This week I want to thank God for...
- This week I want to serve others by...
- This week when I think of others, I want to remember to pray for...
- The church worker I want to pray for this week is...
- I want to ask God to help me...

Spiritual victory is POSSIBLE. It is ACHIEVED one step of OBEDIENCE after another.

Joshua
Entry 4

Bible Reading

- > Numbers 13:17–23
- > Joshua 14:1–6
- > Joshua 14:7–15
- > Joshua 24:1–13
- > Joshua 24:14–30

Beneath the Surface

Think about **Joshua 24:15** as you *finish* it in the space below.

"And if it seem evil unto you to serve the Lord, choose you this day whom ye will serve; . . . but as for me and my house,

What does this verse tell you about Joshua's character?

Looking Back

The precept from this week's lessons that I want to apply to my life is . . .

I can apply that precept by . . .

Observations

Read **Joshua 14:8**. What do you think Caleb meant when he said that he "wholly followed the LORD"?

Read **Joshua 14:12–13**. What did Caleb ask Joshua to give him for his inheritance?

Read **Joshua 19:49–50**. What was Joshua's inheritance? When did he get it?

If you choose to spend your life serving God, when will you receive the greatest reward?

Read **Joshua 23:14**. As Joshua was speaking to the people, what did he want them to remember about God?

Read **Joshua 24:15**. When Joshua gave his final address to the people, how did he challenge the Israelites?

What choices can you make today to serve the Lord?

Look at **Joshua 1:8** and **11:15** again. How can you be successful in your life?

Joshua

Assemblage Analysis

Analysis 1

Read **Numbers 32:12** and **Hebrews 11:24–25**. In what important way were Joshua and Moses alike?

How can you be like Joshua and Moses?

Analysis 2

How did Achan's sin affect Israel?

Israel had to deal with the sin in order to have victory. How does sin affect your life?

What must you do to have spiritual victory?

Analysis 3

Read Joshua 1:5. What promise did God give to Joshua?

Read Hebrews 13:8. Is the God that you know the same God Moses and Joshua served?

When you get discouraged, remember that as God was with Moses and Joshua so He is with you. Think about the last part of Joshua 1:5 and make it personal. Fill in the blanks changing *I* to "God" and *thee* to "me."

As ______________ was with Moses, so ______________ will be with ______________: ______________ will not fail ______________, nor forsake ______________.

Analysis 4

Read 1 Corinthians 2:5. Name one time Joshua put his faith in God's power, not in man's wisdom.

Name another person in the Bible who put his faith in God's power.

Creative Writing

Choose an event in the life of Joshua to write about. Simply retell Joshua's experience in your own words. You, the author, will not refer to yourself or be included.

For example, you would write something like this:

Joshua looked up at Jericho's large wall. It was so high! But God had promised to give Israel victory. All they had to do was obey.

continue on next page

Profile Drawing

Try sketching an illustration of your story in the space below.

Code Word

Use the code to find the promise God gave to Joshua.

A	B	C	D	E	F	G	H	I	J	K	L	M
1	2	3	4	5	6	7	8	9	10	11	12	13
N	**O**	**P**	**Q**	**R**	**S**	**T**	**U**	**V**	**W**	**X**	**Y**	**Z**
14	15	16	17	18	19	20	21	22	23	24	25	26

. . . 1 19   9   23 1 19   23 9 20 8

13 15 19 5 19,   19 15   9   23 9 12 12

2 5   23 9 20 8   20 8 5 5:   9

23 9 12 12   14 15 20   6 1 9 12

20 8 5 5,   14 15 18   6 15 18 19 1 11 5

20 8 5 5.   *Joshua 1:5*

Unscramble the letters to discover what Joshua needed to conquer the land of Canaan.

________________ g s t n e h t r

________________ r o e c g a u

________________ s c s e u c s

Judges

Chosen by God

Judges
Entry 1

Bible Reading

- > Judges 2:6–23
- > Judges 3:7–15, 30–31
- > Judges 4:1–10; 5:1–7
- > Judges 6:1–20
- > Judges 6:21–40

Beneath the Surface

Think about **Psalm 119:125** as you copy it in the space below.

What can you ask God to give you as you read His Word?

Looking Back

The precept from this week's lessons that I want to apply to my life is . . .

I can apply that precept by . . .

Observations

When the Israelites did not know God, they turned to idols. What might people turn to in place of God today?

Read **1 John 1:9**. Why did God constantly forgive the Israelites when they repented?

Is knowing that God will forgive you an excuse to sin?

Read **Judges 2:18**. Whom did God send to the Israelites when they repented of their sin?

The Israelites were influenced by the people around them. Read **Proverbs 27:17**. Describe the influence you and your friends have on each other.

Read **Judges 5:20–21**. What did God use to help Barak defeat Sisera's army?

Read **Judges 6:1–2**. What kept the Israelites from having victory over the Midianites?

Does Satan want you to have spiritual victory in your life?

What are some things that might keep you from having spiritual victory in your life?

Read **Judges 6:7–8**. When did God send a prophet to Israel?

What should you do if you begin to be overwhelmed by things of the world?

Read **Judges 6:25–26**. What was the first thing Gideon had to do?

Daily Living

- This week I want to thank God for...
- This week I want to serve others by...
- This week when I think of others, I want to remember to pray for...
- The government official I want to pray for this week is...
- I want to ask God to help me...

GREATER IS HE that is in you, than he that is in the world.
1 John 4:4

Judges
Entry 2

Bible Reading

- Judges 7:1–14
- Judges 7:15–22
- Judges 13:8–21
- Judges 14:1–9
- Judges 14:12–20

Beneath the Surface

Think about **Judges 7:2** as you copy it in the space below.

Why did God want Gideon to have a smaller army?

Looking Back

The precept from this week's lessons that I want to apply to my life is . . .

I can apply that precept by . . .

Observations

Read **Judges 7:7**. Why did God tell Gideon to take only 300 men with him to defeat the Midianites?

Read **Judges 13:5**. The angel told Manoah's wife that her son would be a ________________.

What did Manoah name his son?

Read **Judges 14:1–2**. Whenever you begin to go your own way instead of walking with God, what direction do you go spiritually?

Samson told his parents, "I have ________________ a woman in Timnath." What should Samson have been guarding?

Was Samson concerned that the woman was a Philistine who did not know God?

Why should Samson have considered what his parents thought?

Read **Exodus 20:12**. How can you honor your father and mother with your choice of friends?

How did the men of Timnath finally figure out the answer to Samson's riddle?

Read **Judges 14:6, 19**. When did Samson receive his great strength?

Read **Isaiah 41:10**. Where does your spiritual strength come from?

cutting shears

Daily Living

- This week I want to thank God for...
- This week I want to serve others by...
- This week when I think of others, I want to remember to pray for...
- The friend I want to pray for this week is...
- I want to ask God to help me...

Do not follow the crowd.

FOLLOW GOD!

Judges
Entry 3

Bible Reading

- > Judges 15:1–5, 7–8
- > Judges 15:9–15
- > Judges 16:4–14
- > Judges 16:15–22
- > Judges 16:23–31

Beneath the Surface

Think about **Judges 16:22** as you copy it in the space below.

How did God show grace to Samson?

Looking Back

The precept from this week's lessons that I want to apply to my life is . . .

I can apply that precept by . . .

Observations

What should Samson have done the first time Delilah tricked him?

Read **Judges 16:20**. Samson's pride led to his capture. What things did Samson end up losing?

Read **Judges 16:28**. What did he want to accomplish in his death?

Do you think that Samson ever really understood his sin? Why or why not?

Analysis 1

Think about Gideon and Samson. Which of these two men was confident in his own strength?

Which of these men was not confident in his own strength but learned to depend on God's strength?

Read John 15:5. What lesson did Samson need to learn?

Read Philippians 4:13. What lesson did Gideon need to learn?

Analysis 2

When God uses ordinary people to do His work, what does that show to the world?

Read Isaiah 6:8. God needs strong leaders that are dependent on Him. Are you willing to ask God to use you?

Analysis 3

What natural abilities has God given you that He can use in His work?

How can you have a balance between developing your abilities and not becoming dependent only on your abilities?

Analysis 4

How might Samson's life have ended differently if he had guarded his eyes and his heart?

Which judge's life story is most memorable to you? Why?

Creative Writing

Choose an event in the life of one of the judges to write about. Simply retell the judge's experience in your own words. You, the author, will not refer to yourself or be included.

For example, you would write something like this:

One day Deborah sat under her favorite palm tree. God had given her a message for Barak, the leader of Israel's army; and she was waiting for him to arrive.

continue on next page

Profile Drawing

Try sketching an illustration of your story in the space below.

Also I heard the voice of the

Lord,

saying,

Whom shall I send, and who will go for Us?

Then said I,

Here am I; send me.

Isaiah 6:8

Ruth

Seeker of God

Ruth
Entry 1

Bible Reading

- > Ruth 1:1–7, 14–21
- > Ruth 2:1–17
- > Ruth 2:18–23
- > Ruth 3:1–2, 11–18
- > Ruth 4:1–9

Beneath the Surface

Think about **Ruth 1:16** as you copy it in the space below.

Do you think this was an easy choice for Ruth?

Looking Back

The precept from this week's lessons that I want to apply to my life is . . .

I can apply that precept by . . .

Observations

Read **Ruth 1:1–2**. Why did Elimelech and Naomi decide to go to Moab?

Would God have taken care of them if they had stayed in Bethlehem?

How you react to difficult things or times reveals much about you. Read **Isaiah 41:10** and **1 Corinthians 9:24**. What will you choose to do when difficulties come?

Read **Ruth 1:6**. Why did Naomi return to the land of Judah?

Read Ruth 1:20. What did Naomi tell the people to call her when she returned to Bethlehem?

Why do you think she chose this name?

Read Ruth 2:3. What does "her hap was to light" mean?

Who directed Ruth to that particular field?

Read Ruth 2:11–12. What did Boaz recognize about Ruth?

Read Ruth 2:16. How were the actions of Boaz similar to God's actions toward His children?

Read Ruth 2:20. What did Naomi finally recognize about God?

Read Ruth 3:11. What was Ruth's testimony among the people of Judah?

Many years later, Solomon, one of Ruth's descendants, wrote about the virtuous woman. Read Proverbs 31:10. How did Solomon describe her worth?

Interesting Fact: Ruth is the only woman described in the Bible as virtuous.

Read Ruth 4:14–15. How did God use Ruth to bless Naomi?

How might God bless others through you?

Ruth
Assemblage Analysis

Analysis 1

Read **Ruth 4:9**. Boaz paid the price to become the kinsman redeemer. What price did God pay to become your Redeemer?

Analysis 2

In what ways did Ruth show her care for Naomi?

How can you show care for your family members?

Analysis 3

Read **Ruth 4:17**. Ruth was rewarded by becoming the great-grandmother of which king of Israel?

How else was Ruth rewarded?

What do you think was Ruth's greatest reward?

Analysis 4

Ruth had many good character traits such as kindness, diligence, and obedience. Name one way that Ruth's character helped her have a good testimony to those around her.

Name one way you could have a good testimony.

Creative Writing

Pretend that you are one of the people in the story of Ruth. Choose an event in the life of Ruth and write what you would think, do, or say during that event. Remember to use the words *I* and *we* to write from this point of view.

For example, you would write something like this:

Being away from home is hard, but I know Naomi needs me. I will work hard to provide for our family.

continue on next page

Profile Drawing

Try sketching an illustration of your story in the space below.

Flag It Down

Decode the answers.

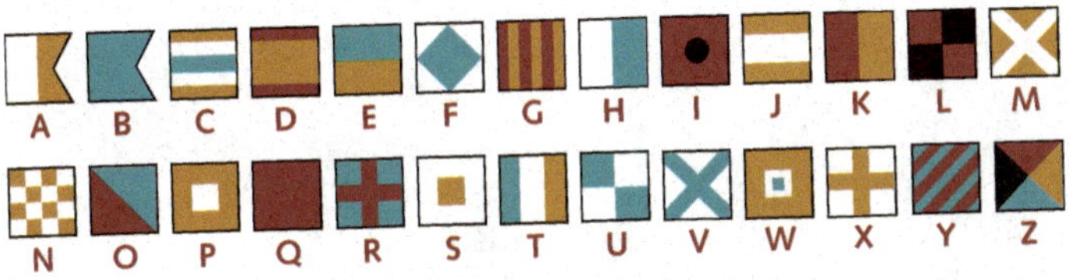

She became Ruth's mother-in-law.

She chose to stay in her homeland.

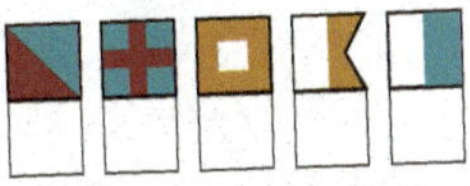

He became Ruth's kinsman redeemer.

She left her homeland to care for her mother-in-law.

Naomi temporarily lived here.

Naomi wanted to be called this name.

Naomi lived here in Israel.

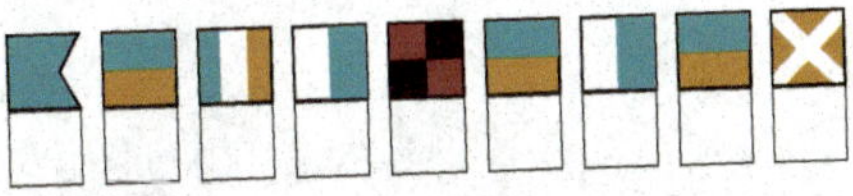

He was the husband of Naomi.

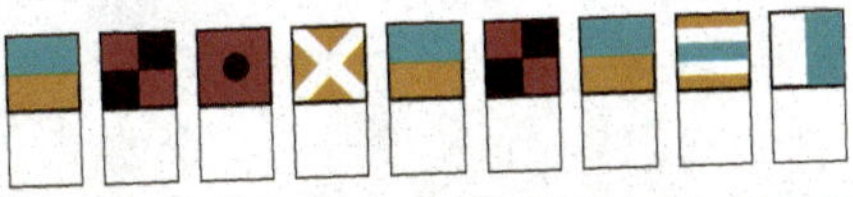

Jonah

Runner from God

Jonah
Entry 1

Bible Reading

- > Jonah 1:1–17
- > Jonah 2:1–10
- > Jonah 3:1–10
- > Jonah 4:1–11
- > Psalm 139:1–18

Beneath the Surface

Think about **Psalm 139:7** as you copy it in the space below.

Are you ever out of God's presence?

Looking Back

The precept from this week's lessons that I want to apply to my life is . . .

I can apply that precept by . . .

Observations

Read **Jonah 1:2–3**. Where did God tell Jonah to go?

According to verse 3, what was Jonah fleeing from?

Read **Jeremiah 23:24**. Could he have ever been successful in trying to flee? Why or why not?

Read **Jonah 1:5**. How did the mariners or sailors try to help themselves?

Why do you think Jonah could sleep so soundly during the storm?

Read **Jonah 1:9–11**. Why do you think that the men were so fearful when Jonah told them Whom he worshiped?

When they realized the storm was a result of Jonah's disobedience, what did they ask him?

Even though there was a great storm, Jonah was still determined not to obey. Read **Jonah 1:12**. What did he tell the mariners to do?

Why do you think God allowed Jonah to be swallowed by a great fish rather than die?

Could God have sent someone else to Nineveh?

If you had been on the ship with Jonah and you did not want to see him thrown overboard, what might have you said to him to convince him to obey God?

Do you tell yourself the same thing when you are about to disobey?

Why do you think that Jonah waited three days in the belly of the fish to pray?

Why do you sometimes wait?

Read Jonah 3:10. How was God's response to the repentance of the people of Nineveh different from Jonah's response?

How should you respond to God's love and forgiveness to someone who has been unkind to you?

Jonah

Assemblage Analysis

Analysis 1

Noah warned the people of judgment for 120 years and no one repented. Jonah warned the people of Nineveh for a few days and the city was saved. Read Psalm 86:15 and Jonah 4:2. What was true about God in both instances?

According to Mark 16:15, what does God command you to tell everyone about Jesus?

Analysis 2

Name one way that Jonah and the people of Nineveh were similar.

Name one way they were different.

Analysis 3

Read Jonah 4:4–5. What did God ask Jonah?

After Jonah told the people about judgment, what do you think Jonah was still hoping to see?

Have you ever been so angry with someone that even though he said he was sorry, you still wanted him to be in trouble? Do you ever try to justify your response of anger by saying, "Well, he did this first"?

Read Luke 23:34. How could you be like Jesus?

Analysis 4

Read Jonah 4:10–11. What was God trying to teach Jonah about His love?

What did you learn about God's love?

Creative Writing

Choose an event in the life of Jonah to write about. Simply retell Jonah's experience in your own words. You, the author, will not refer to yourself or be included.

For example, you would write something like this:

Jonah sat in darkness, surrounded by the smell of dead fish. In his heart, he asked God to forgive him for his disobedience.

continue on next page

Profile Drawing

Try sketching an illustration of your story in the space below.

The LORD
is merciful
and gracious,
slow to anger,
and plenteous
in mercy.
Psalm 103:8

Life of Samuel

Given to God

Life of Samuel
Entry 1

Bible Reading

- 1 Samuel 1:1–8
- 1 Samuel 1:9–28
- 1 Samuel 2:1–11
- 1 Samuel 4:3–17
- 1 Samuel 10:17–26

Beneath the Surface

Think about **1 Samuel 1:28** as you copy it in the space below.

How did Hannah honor God when He gave her Samuel?

Looking Back

The precept from this week's lessons that I want to apply to my life is . . .

I can apply that precept by . . .

Observations

Read 1 Samuel 1:11. Hannah desired something that only God could provide. What did Hannah pray for?

Read 1 Samuel 1:17–18. When Hannah heard that her request would be answered, how did she react?

How did this reaction show Hannah's faith that God would answer her prayer?

What did Hannah promise God if He would give her a son?

Read Psalm 139:17–18. Why can you trust God to do what is best for you?

Read 1 Samuel 4:3. What were the people of Israel putting their faith in to help them win the battle?

Can an object ever replace God?

Going to church is important because God commands us to assemble together. Should attending church ever replace your personal time with God?
Why or why not?

Read 1 Samuel 5:2–3. When the Philistines took the Ark, where did they place it?

What happened to the god of the Philistines?

Read 1 Samuel 9:21. Did Saul think of himself as important when Samuel first met him?

Read 1 Samuel 10:21–23. When Samuel went to anoint Saul king, where did the people find Saul?

Daily Living

- This week I want to thank God for...
- This week I want to serve others by...
- This week when I think of others, I want to remember to pray for...
- The missionary I want to pray for this week is...
- I want to ask God to help me...

Never be afraid that your prayer is TOO BIG for God.

Life of Samuel

Entry 2

Bible Reading

- 1 Samuel 13:1–15
- 1 Samuel 14:1–18
- 1 Samuel 14:24–30, 38–46
- 1 Samuel 15:1–3, 7–23
- 1 Samuel 15:24–35

Beneath the Surface

Think about **1 Samuel 15:22** as you copy it in the space below.

What is one way that you can show your love for God?

Looking Back

The precept from this week's lessons that I want to apply to my life is . . .

I can apply that precept by . . .

Observations

Read 1 Samuel 13:8–12. What did Saul do that only the Levites were to do?

Read 1 Samuel 15:19–21. When Samuel clearly told Saul that he had not obeyed, how did Saul respond the second time?

When you are confronted about your sin, how do you respond? Do you give excuses as Saul did?

What was the result of Saul's disobedience?

Assemblage Analysis

Analysis 1

Samuel started out well and ended well. Throughout his life, how did his humility help him to serve the Lord?

Analysis 2

Saul started out well and, like Samuel, showed great humility. What changed in Saul's heart that caused him not to end well?

How can you guard against this happening in your life?

Analysis 3

Read 1 Samuel 15:35. Why do you think Samuel mourned for Saul?

How does mourning for Saul show Samuel's humility?

Analysis 4

What lessons did you learn from Samuel?

Creative Writing

Choose an event in the life of Samuel to write about. Simply retell Samuel's experience in your own words. You, the author, will not refer to yourself or be included.

For example, you would write something like this:

Samuel walked slowly away from the people. "God is our king," he thought. "Why do the people want an earthly king?"

continue on next page

Profile Drawing

Try sketching an illustration of your story in the space below.

Color Blocks

As a young boy, Samuel learned to obey God's voice. Because of his obedience, God made Samuel one of the greatest judges in Israel. Samuel taught the Israelites about God's faithfulness and righteousness as he encouraged them to serve and obey.

Follow the directions to color the puzzle. When the puzzle is colored, you will find the answer to the following question: **Based on the lessons, how would you describe Samuel's character?**

	1	2	3	4	5	6	7	8	9	10	11	12	13	14	15	16	17	18	19	20	21	22	23	24	25
A																									
B																									
C																									
D																									
E																									

Color these blocks **yellow**:

A–15, 16, 17
B–15, 17
C–15, 16
D–15, 17
E–15, 16, 17

Color these blocks **blue**:

A–1, 3
B–1, 3
C–1, 2, 3
D–1, 3
E–1, 3

Color these blocks **orange**:

A–23, 24, 25
B–23
C–23, 24
D–23
E–23, 24, 25

Color these blocks **red**:

A–9, 13
B–9, 10, 12, 13
C–9, 11, 13
D–9, 13
E–9, 13

Color these blocks **brown**:

A–19
B–19
C–19
D–19
E–19, 20, 21

Color these blocks **purple**:

A–5, 7
B–5, 7
C–5, 7
D–5, 7
E–5, 6, 7

Easter

Sacrifice of God

Easter
Entry 1

Bible Reading

- > Matthew 26:3–25
- > Matthew 26:26–44
- > Matthew 26:45–67
- > Matthew 27:29–53
- > Matthew 28:1–20

Beneath the Surface

Think about **Mark 16:6** as you copy it in the space below.

What two important facts do you know about Jesus from this verse?

Looking Back

The precept from this week's lessons that I want to apply to my life is . . .

I can apply that precept by . . .

Observations

Read **Mark 15:37–39**. What words in these verses tell you that Jesus was in control of His death?

What did the centurion say when he saw Jesus die on the cross?

Why did Jesus die on the cross?

Read John 19:30. What was finished when Jesus gave up His life on the cross?

Paul wrote about the "power of the resurrection." Read Philippians 3:10. What does that mean to you?

How can that power help you live a godly life?

Do you ask God for that power each day?

Read Mark 16:7. Why did Jesus send Peter a special message that He wanted to see him?

What important lesson do you think Peter learned through the death and resurrection of Jesus?

Daily Living

- This week I want to thank God for...
- This week I want to serve others by...
- This week when I think of others, I want to remember to pray for...
- The first responders I want to pray for this week are...
- I want to ask God to help me...

GIVE your life to God. He gave His Son FOR YOU.

What Easter Means to Me

Life of David
Heart of God

Life of David
Entry 1

Bible Reading

- > *1 Samuel 16:1–13*
- > *1 Samuel 17:21–37*
- > *1 Samuel 17:38–50*
- > *1 Samuel 18:1–11; 19:1–10*
- > *1 Samuel 20:1–16*

Beneath the Surface

Think about 1 Samuel 16:7 as you *finish* the verse in the space below.

"But the LORD said unto Samuel, Look not on his countenance, or on the height of his stature; because I have refused him: for the LORD seeth not as man seeth;

What should you consider when choosing a friend?

Looking Back

The precept from this week's lessons that I want to apply to my life is . . .

I can apply that precept by . . .

Observations

Read 1 Samuel 16:1–2. What did God tell Samuel to do?

Why was Samuel afraid to go to Bethlehem to anoint a new king?

Read 1 Samuel 16:6–10. Why do you think Jesse did not call David as soon as Samuel arrived?

When Samuel sent for David, he was with the sheep. What do you think this shows about David?

Read **1 Samuel 16:18**. How was David described in this verse?

Read **1 Samuel 16:21–23**. What did David's music do for Saul?

Read **1 Samuel 17:20, 22**. What do these two verses tell you about David?

Read **1 Samuel 17:23–24**. Why were the men of Israel afraid to fight Goliath?

Read **1 Samuel 17:28**. How did David's brother react to David's asking about Goliath?

Why did David refuse to wear Saul's armor?

Read 1 Samuel 17:37. What gave David confidence to fight Goliath?

Who became David's good friend?

What did Jonathan give to David when he heard that David would be the next king?

Read 1 Samuel 20:14–15. What promise did David make to Jonathan?

Life of David
Assemblage Analysis

Analysis 1

Read 1 Samuel 17:29–30. What important question did David ask Eliab?

Read 1 Samuel 17:45. What was the cause that gave David the courage to face Goliath?

How can you stand for God today?

Analysis 2

Read 1 Samuel 17:41. Who went with Goliath to meet David?

Who went with David to meet Goliath?

Victory is rarely easy. It takes commitment and the right weapons. Read 1 Corinthians 15:57. How can you have victory over sin?

Analysis 3

David was given an opportunity that Jonathan probably expected to have. How do you react when someone is given the opportunity to do something that you wanted for yourself?

Analysis 4

Read 1 Samuel 17:33. Saul should have been encouraged by David's words, but did his pride allow it?

Read 1 Samuel 18:4. How do you think that the actions of Jonathan encouraged David?

What actions could you take to encourage someone who is serving the Lord?

Creative Writing

Pretend you are David. Write what you would think, do, or say when you face Goliath. Remember to use the words *I* and *we* to write from this point of view.

For example, you would write something like this:

I reached for my sling and chose one stone. The giant stood tall several yards away, but I felt God's peace in my heart.

continue on next page

Profile Drawing

Try sketching an illustration of your story in the space below.

And *David* behaved himself *wisely* in all his ways; and the *LORD* was with him.

1 Samuel 18:14

Life of David
Entry 2

Bible Reading

- > 1 Samuel 21:6–15
- > 1 Samuel 24:1–22
- > 1 Samuel 25:4–16, 27–31
- > 1 Samuel 27:1–12
- > 1 Samuel 29:1–11

Beneath the Surface

Think about **Psalm 18:3** as you copy it in the space below.

Why is God worthy of praise?

Looking Back

The precept from this week's lessons that I want to apply to my life is . . .

I can apply that precept by . . .

Observations

Read **1 Samuel 22:1–2**. How does the Bible describe the men who came to join David in the cave of Adullam?

David sought God's direction, and God guided and protected him. Read **1 Samuel 23:26–28**. How did God rescue David when Saul's army was beginning to surround him?

Read **1 Samuel 24:6**. Why did David refuse to harm Saul?

Read 1 Samuel 25:14–17. How did God protect David from harming Nabal?

Do you think Abigail was nervous going to David?

Read Proverbs 15:1. What was one biblical principle Abigail followed when she approached David?

God called David a man after His own heart. Yet even David became discouraged and had a lack of faith. Read 1 Samuel 27:1. What poor decision did David make while he was discouraged?

King Achish gave David the town of Ziklag. Do you think that David was comfortable at Ziklag?
Why or why not?

Read 1 Samuel 30:6–10. What did the people talk about doing to David when they returned to Ziklag and found their families gone?

What did David do?

While some men stayed at the brook, why do you think David continued confidently with only 400 men?

Brook of Besor

Daily Living

- This week I want to thank God for...
- This week I want to serve others by...
- This week when I think of others, I want to remember to pray for...
- The family member I want to pray for this week is...
- I want to ask God to help me...

Never be afraid to SPEAK UP when helping a friend make RIGHT CHOICES.

Life of David
Entry 3

Bible Reading

> 1 Samuel 28:3–14
> 1 Samuel 28:15–25
> 1 Samuel 31:1–7, 11–13
> 2 Samuel 1:1–12
> 2 Samuel 1:17–27

Beneath the Surface

Think about **Psalm 16:8** as you copy it in the space below.

What was the source of David's confidence?

Looking Back

The precept from this week's lessons that I want to apply to my life is . . .

I can apply that precept by . . .

Observations

What happened to Saul and his sons in the battle against the Philistines?

Read **2 Samuel 1:11–12**. What was David's reaction to the death of Saul and Jonathan and the defeat of Israel?

How might Saul's life have ended differently if he had repented of his sin?

God's love for you never changes even when you sin, yet it is important that you repent when you sin. Why?

Life of David

Assemblage Analysis

Analysis 1

Read 1 Samuel 22:8. When Saul was upset, whom did he focus on?

Read Psalm 57:1–2. When David fled from Saul, Whom did he focus on?

When difficulties come, what can you do to keep your focus or thoughts right?

Analysis 2

Read 1 Samuel 23:16–17. How did God encourage David when he was running from Saul?

Read 1 Samuel 30:6. How did David encourage himself?

How might memorized Scripture encourage you?

Analysis 3

How did David react when Nabal refused his request for food?

Saul had done more to David than Nabal had done. Why do you think David reacted so differently to Nabal than he did to Saul?

Why is it important to have the right reactions?

Analysis 4

How might you have reacted to Saul's death if you had been one of David's men?

Read 2 Samuel 1:11–12. What example did David set for the people of Israel when Saul died?

Creative Writing

Write a selection comparing and contrasting Saul and David. Write a paragraph of similarities and a paragraph of differences. You may choose to use some of these signal words:

however, both, although, different, similar, alike

continue on next page

Profile Drawing

Try sketching an illustration of your comparison in the space below.

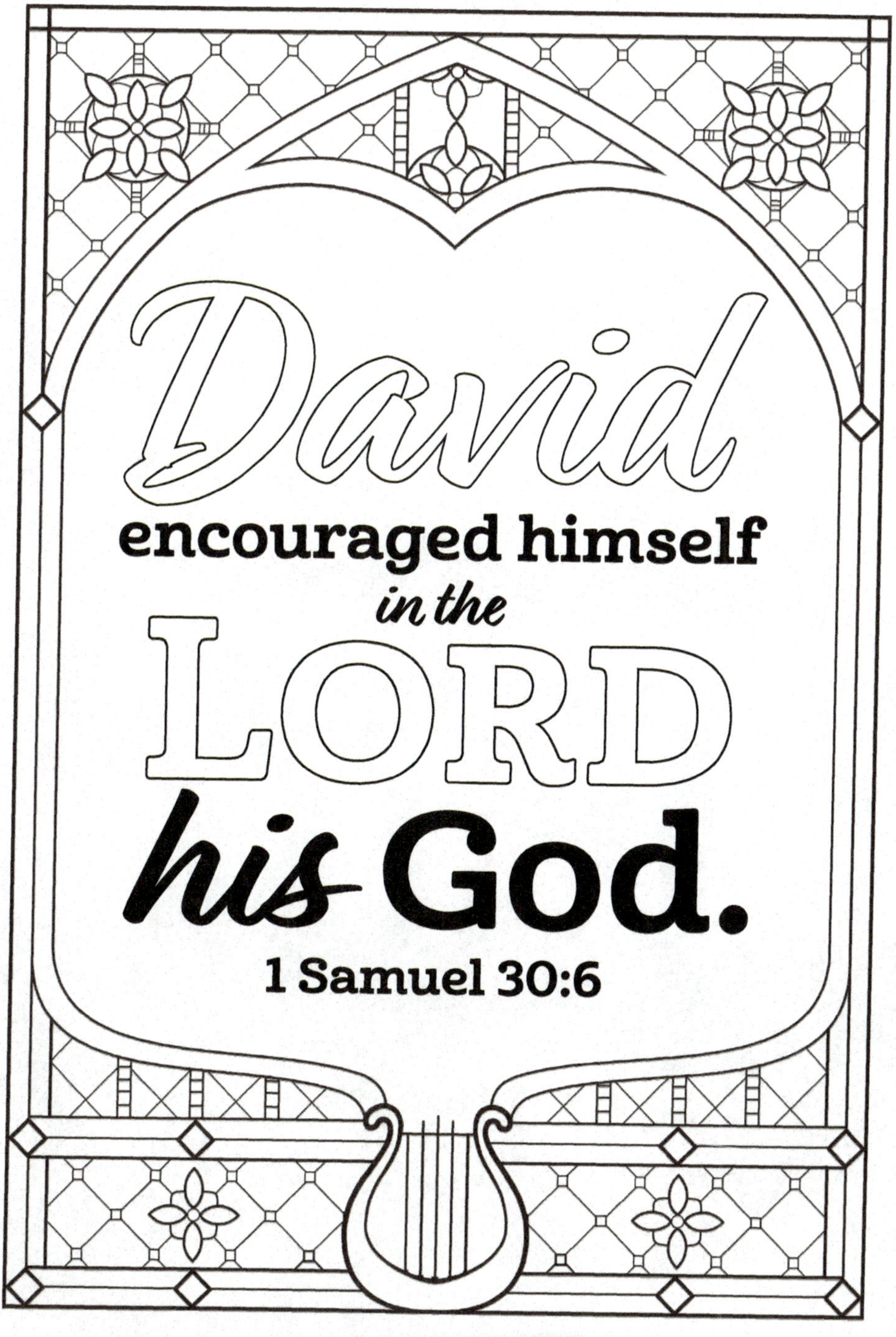
David
encouraged himself
in the
LORD
his God.
1 Samuel 30:6

Life of David

Entry 4

Bible Reading

- 2 Samuel 2:1–11
- 2 Samuel 3:1–2, 17–25
- 2 Samuel 5:1–5, 17–25
- 2 Samuel 7:1–11, 18–22
- 2 Samuel 9:1–13

Beneath the Surface

Think about **Psalm 27:14** as you copy it in the space below.

What is one way that you can wait on God?

Looking Back

The precept from this week's lessons that I want to apply to my life is . . .

I can apply that precept by . . .

Observations

Read **2 Samuel 2:1, 4**. After Saul died, what did David do before moving his men and family to a new location?

What did the men of Judah do after David arrived in Hebron?

Read **2 Samuel 3:12**. What did Abner, the captain of Saul's army, agree to do for David?

Read **2 Samuel 3:31–32**. How did David respond to the death of Abner?

Read 2 Samuel 5:4–5. How long did David reign as king over all Israel and Judah?

Read 2 Samuel 6:2–3. When David wanted to bring up the Ark of the Covenant to the city of Jerusalem, what did the people use to move it?

Why do you think there was such a great celebration when the Ark of the Covenant was brought to Jerusalem?

How does your relationship with God affect how you think, feel, and act?

Read 2 Samuel 9:6–7. Who was Mephibosheth?

What promise did David give to Mephibosheth?

Daily Living

- This week I want to thank God for...
- This week I want to serve others by...
- This week when I think of others, I want to remember to pray for...
- The church worker I want to pray for this week is...
- I want to ask God to help me...

As shepherd and as king, David SOUGHT the PRESENCE of God.

Life of David

Entry 5

Bible Reading

- 2 Samuel 11:1, 22–27
- 2 Samuel 12:1–9, 13–23
- 2 Samuel 14:21–33
- 2 Samuel 15:1–12
- 2 Samuel 16:1–4; 19:24–30

Beneath the Surface

Think about **Psalm 51:4** as you copy it in the space below.

Why is it impossible to hide sin from God?

Looking Back

The precept from this week's lessons that I want to apply to my life is . . .

I can apply that precept by . . .

Observations

Read **2 Samuel 11:1**. When David should have been leading his men in battle, where did he stay?

First, David was in the wrong place, and then he looked at the wrong thing. Read **Psalm 101:3**. Why is it important for you to continually guard where you go and what you see?

Instead of confessing his sin, what did David try to do?

Who confronted David about his sin?

Read **2 Samuel 12:13**. How did David react when his sin became known?

David confessed his sin and was forgiven, but he still had consequences. Does confessing sin take away the consequences of sin?

Read **2 Samuel 15:2–6**. How did Absalom subtly work on turning the people from his father David and winning them over to himself?

Read **1 Timothy 2:1–2**. Do you think it is wise to listen to someone who talks disrespectfully against authority? Why or why not?

Read **2 Samuel 15:25–26**. How did David show his faith in God as he was leaving Jerusalem?

Daily Living

- This week I want to thank God for...

- This week I want to serve others by...

- This week when I think of others, I want to remember to pray for...

- The friend I want to pray for this week is...

- I want to ask God to help me...

Absalom sought the HEARTS of the PEOPLE. David sought the HEART of GOD.

Life of David

Entry 6

Bible Reading

- 1 Kings 1:28–36
- 1 Kings 1:37–45
- 1 Kings 2:1–4, 10–12
- 1 Chronicles 22:1–6
- 1 Chronicles 22:11–19

Beneath the Surface

Think about **Psalm 27:1** as you copy it in the space below.

David put his confidence in the Lord. Where is your confidence?

Looking Back

The precept from this week's lessons that I want to apply to my life is . . .

I can apply that precept by . . .

Observations

Read **1 Kings 2:45**. What had God promised David about his family?

Read **Luke 1:32–33**. David's throne was going to be established forever because he would be the ancestor of Whom?

Read **2 Samuel 23:1**. Because David wrote many of the Psalms, what did the people of Israel call him?

David had a desire to build a great house for the Lord, but that was not God's plan. Read **2 Samuel 7:25–29**. How did David respond to God's plan for the Temple and for his family?

If you had a strong desire to do something and you were told no, how should you respond?

Even though David was not permitted to build a house unto the name of God, he did what he could. Read **1 Chronicles 22:2–5**. What did David do for Solomon to help Solomon build a house for God?

David asked God to give Solomon wisdom and understanding. Why was this a good thing to pray for Solomon?

This is a good prayer for yourself and others. Whom could you ask God to give wisdom and understanding to in your home?

Your church?

Your community?

Read **1 Chronicles 22:16**. What did David tell Solomon to do?

When you are given a job to do, why is it important to get started as soon as possible?

David commanded the princes of Israel to help Solomon. What are some ways that you can help your community?

Analysis 1

Read 2 Samuel 9:7–8, 10. What did David promise to Mephibosheth?

After Mephibosheth met King David, he ate at the king's table the rest of his life. Did Mephibosheth do anything to earn the promise of David?

David was fulfilling his promise to Jonathan. All Mephibosheth had to do was accept the free gift. Once you accept the free gift of salvation, God will keep His promise to you of eternal life in Heaven with Him. Name one other promise God has given to you.

Analysis 2

Samuel anointed David to be king over all of Israel. After the death of Saul, he reigned seven years over Judah. What might have happened if David had not waited and had declared himself king of Israel instead?

What did you learn about waiting on God's direction and timing?

Analysis 3

Read Psalm 55:17. What had David learned to do throughout his life?

Look carefully at the verse. Did David say that God *might* hear his voice, or *sometimes* hears his voice?

David was confident that God would ____________ hear his voice.

Do you believe that God *will* hear your voice whenever you pray?

Analysis 4

David was the only person in the Bible described as a man after God's own heart. Explain what it means to be a man after God's own heart.

Could you be described as having a heart after God's own heart?

Creative Writing

Choose an event in the life of David to write about. Simply retell David's experience in your own words. You, the author, will not refer to yourself or be included. For example, you would write something like this:

David knew that Absalom was meeting with the people as they came into the city. At first, he was proud of Absalom for being a leader. However, he realized too late that Absalom had betrayed him.

continue on next page

Profile Drawing

Try sketching an illustration of your story in the space below.

Connect the Dots

Connect the dots to see a description of David.

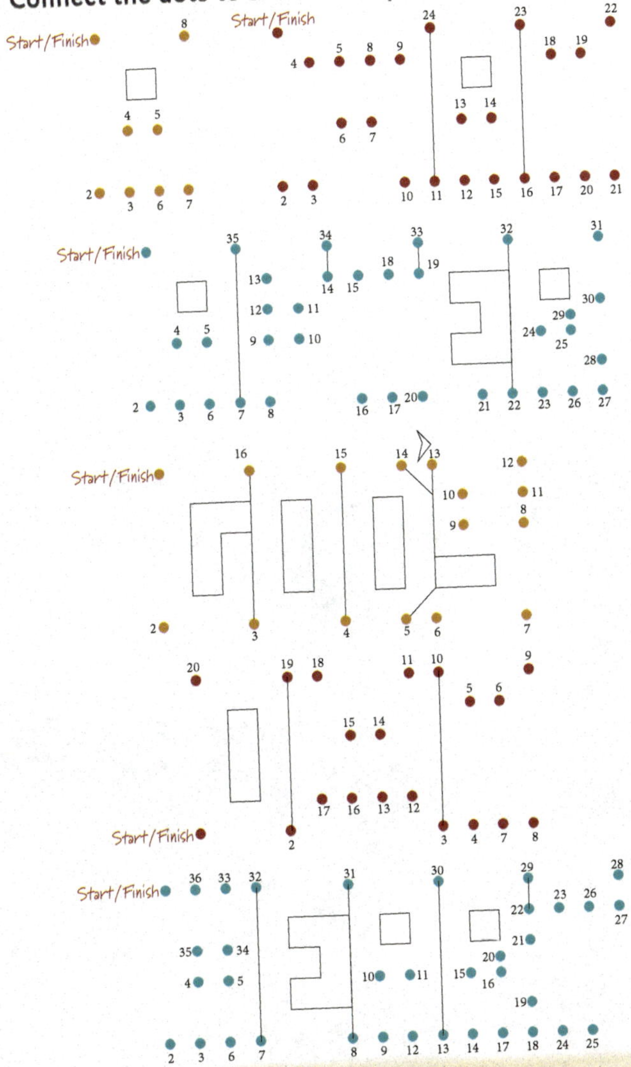

Optional Activities

God's Plan of Salvation

Would you know what to tell a friend if he asked you how to go to Heaven? Write out what you would say to your friend. Explain why your friend needs a savior, why God sent a Savior, Who the Savior is, and what your friend must do to receive God's gift of the Savior. Include a Bible verse you might use for each.

continue on next page

My Testimony

One way to tell people about Jesus is by sharing what happened to you when you asked Jesus to be your Savior. This is called a testimony. You may have the opportunity to share your testimony. Do you know what you would say? In the space provided, write your own testimony about how you received Jesus as your Savior.

continue on next page

Lessons Learned

As you are learning many lessons throughout the year and are studying God's Word for yourself, the Bible will change you. Look for attributes of God that help you. Think about how you can establish some good habits that will help you to continue to grow spiritually. Consider the lessons you are learning and their effect on your life today. Keep track of the important decisions you make throughout the year by writing them down.

For example, you would write something like this:

When God told Moses to lead the Israelites out of Egypt, Moses told God that he could not speak well. I learned that God has a job for me and He will give me exactly what I need to do that job.

continue on next page

10
solutions pour accroître l'estime de soi

Une méthode simple
pour apprendre à mieux vous apprécier.

GLENN R. SCHIRALDI, Ph. D.,

Broquet
97-B, Montée des Bouleaux, Saint-Constant, Qc, Canada, J5A 1A9
Tél.: 450 638-3338 Téléc.: 450 638-4338
Internet: www.broquet.qc.ca Courriel: info@broquet.qc.ca

Catalogage avant publication de Bibliothèque et Archives nationales du Québec et Bibliothèque et Archives Canada

Schiraldi, Glenn R., 1947-

10 solutions pour accroître l'estime de soi

Traduction de : 10 simple solutions for building self-esteem.

ISBN 978-2-89654-076-1

1. Estime de soi. 2. Confiance en soi. I. Titre. II. Titre : Dix solutions pour accroître l'estime de soi.

BF697.5.S46S3414 2009 158.1 C2009-940643-8

POUR L'AIDE À LA RÉALISATION DE SON PROGRAMME ÉDITORIAL, L'ÉDITEUR REMERCIE :
le gouvernement du Canada par l'entremise du Programme d'aide au développement de l'industrie de l'édition (PADIÉ) ; la Société de développement des entreprises culturelles (SODEC) ; l'Association pour l'exportation du livre canadien (AELC).
Le gouvernement du Québec – Programme de crédit d'impôt pour l'édition de livres – Gestion SODEC.

Titre original : *10 Simple Solutions for Building Self-Esteem*

New Harbinger Publications, Inc.
5674 Shattuck Avenue
Oakland, CA 94609
www.newharbinger.com

Dépôt légal – Bibliothèque et Archives nationales du Québec
2e trimestre 2009

Traduction : Claude Dallaire
Révision : Denis Poulet, Diane Martin
Infographie : Nancy Lépine

Imprimé au Canada

ISBN 978-2-89654-076-1

Crédit photographique
Page couverture : © Andrey Popov | iStockphoto.com

Note de l'éditeur
Cette publication a été conçue dans le but de donner des informations justes et documentées à propos du sujet abordé, mais le lecteur comprendra qu'elle ne peut tenir lieu de services psychologiques, financiers, juridiques ou autres. Si vous avez besoin d'aide professionnelle, retenez les services d'un professionnel compétent.

« Méditation pour apprécier votre corps », au chapitre 7, a été légèrement condensée et reproduite avec l'autorisation de Jack Canfield (1985), « Body Appreciation » dans *Wisdom, Purpose and Love.* Copyright 1985, Jack Canfield, coauteur de la série *Chicken Soup for the Soul.* Ne pas reproduire sans autorisation écrite. À l'origine, cette version a été rééditée avec l'autorisation de l'éditeur dans Schiraldi, G. R. *The Self-Esteem Workbook,* Oakland, CA, New Harbinger Publications, 2001.

Les exercices de défusion « Identifiez la source de la douleur », « Lait, lait, lait », « Tenez un journal » et « Emportez-le avec vous » du chapitre 3 ont été adaptés avec l'autorisation de l'éditeur de *Get Out of Your Mind and Into Your Life* de S. C. Hayes et S. Smith, publié par New Harbinger Publications, Oakland, CA en 2005. © détenu par S. C. Hayes et S. Smith, 2005.

L'exercice « La chandelle du pardon » du chapitre 9 a été adapté avec l'autorisation de l'éditeur de *Act on Life Not on Anger* de G. H. Eifert, M. McKay et J. P. Forsyth, publié par New Harbinger Publications, Oakland, CA en 2006. © détenu par G.H. Eifert, M. McKay et J. P. Forsyth, 2006.

La « Parabole des plaquettes de microscope brisées » du chapitre 9 est tirée d'un sermon non publié livré par le révérend P. C. Shupe et adapté avec son autorisation. © détenu par P. C. Shupe, 2006.